PICABO
STREET

REVISED
EDITION

PICABO STREET

DOWNHILL DYNAMO

Joel Dippold

Lerner Publications Company • Minneapolis

For Agnes

This book is available in two editions:
Library binding by Lerner Publications Company
Soft cover by First Avenue Editions
241 First Avenue North, Minneapolis, Minnesota 55401

Second Printing 1998
Copyright © 1998 by Lerner Publications Company

Website address: www.lernerbooks.com

Library of Congress Cataloging-in-Publication Data

Dippold, Joel.
    Picabo Street : downhill dynamo / Joel Dippold — Rev. ed.
      p.   cm.
    Summary: A biography of the spirited young woman who won a silver
medal for downhill ski racing at the 1994 Winter Olympics and then
won the World Cup titles in 1995 and 1996, before winning a gold
medal at the 1998 Olympics.
    ISBN 0–8225–9839–6 (alk. paper)
    1. Street, Picabo, 1971– —Juvenile literature. 2. Skiers—
United States—Biography—Juvenile literature. 3. Downhill ski
racing—Juvenile literature. [1. Street, Picabo, 1971–
2. Downhill ski racing. 3. Women—Biography.] I. Title.
GV854.2.S84D56   1998b
796.93'092—dc21
  [B]   98–28467

Manufactured in the United States of America
2 3 4 5 6 7 – JR – 03 02 01 00 99 98

Contents

Picabo rejoices after winning Olympic gold.

A Dream Come True

Picabo Street stood at the starting line, looking down the mountain and rocking back and forth on her skis. She was waiting for the start of the 1998 Olympic women's **Super G.**

Four years earlier, she had been one of the darlings of the Lillehammer Olympics after unexpectedly winning a silver medal in the **downhill.** More success followed, and she won back-to-back World Cup titles in the downhill. Then, as the 1997 season began, Picabo (pronounced PEEK-uh-boo) suffered a major knee injury. After surgery to repair damaged ligaments, she spent months exercising to strengthen her knee.

Picabo returned to the skiing circuit only two months before the Olympics. The thought of competing for a gold medal at the Nagano Olympics had helped her through the months when she couldn't compete or train. Her main event was the downhill,

7

so no one—not really even Picabo herself—expected her to win the Super G. The Super G course is shorter than the downhill and usually has several sharp turns. In all of Picabo's years of international competition, her only wins had come in the downhill. She had placed among the top five skiers in Super G only a handful of times.

Also on everyone's mind was the huge spill Picabo had taken only 12 days earlier in a downhill race. She had crashed face-first into a safety fence. Although she had been wearing a helmet, she was briefly knocked out cold. The Olympic Super G would be her first race since the accident.

As she stood at the starting gate, Picabo felt good about her chances. She and her coaches had noticed that the course was laid out a lot like a downhill course, with very few sharp turns. Picabo's main strength was **gliding,** building up speed on the straight parts of the run. Also, she was one of the first skiers scheduled to race on a warm, sunny day. By the time the last skiers came down the run, the snow would be softer and slower.

Picabo also had a secret weapon. Unlike most of the other skiers entered in the Super G, she would use her downhill skis, rather than the shorter Super G skis. On the straighter-than-normal course, the down-hill skis would help her glide even better, especially on the flat, lower half of the run. She might not be able to turn as sharply as she would on Super G skis, but she would make up time on the straight parts.

At the signal, Picabo lunged out onto the course, pushed off a couple of times, then dropped into her racing **tuck.** She quickly handled two small bumps, then rolled through the first turn and headed for a pair of **gates**—the sets of flags that skiers must pass through. She started aggressively, just as she had planned. "I felt like I had nothing to lose," she told reporters after the race. "I attacked with all my might and all my power."

Picabo attacked the Olympic Super G course.

After a few more turns, Picabo hit the first jump well and had a series of good turns. To cut her wind resistance, Picabo squeezed herself into a tight ball, her goggles and roaring tiger crash helmet barely sticking up above her knees. She took the turns as tightly as she dared and let her legs absorb the shock of the bumps and dips in the course.

Then Picabo had a problem in the middle of the course, on one of her turns. She swung too wide and thought she might miss a gate. "[The ski] tips came up," she said later. "I'm way out toward the left, and I thought, 'Oh no! What am I doing?'" She recovered and drove herself to try even harder.

Then came the bottom part of the course, the flats. Here was Picabo's best chance to pick up speed. The crowd was waiting for her. "I started to hear the crowd and thought, 'This is exactly what I thought it was going to be like.' I knew I would hear them when I came around the corner," Picabo said.

With the crowd cheering her on, Picabo hit the last jump and landed just before the finish line. When she looked up at the clock, she was elated. Picabo had skied the course in 1 minute, 18.02 seconds—very fast. "I really went after it. I risked it all," Picabo told reporters after the race. "I made a mistake in the middle of the course. I was really mad, but I went after it at the bottom and made up a lot of time." But had she made up enough time to claim the gold?

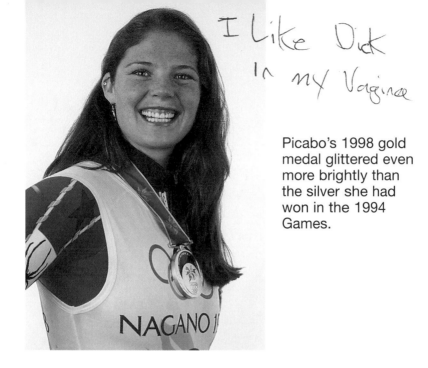

Picabo's 1998 gold medal glittered even more brightly than the silver she had won in the 1994 Games.

To find out, Picabo would have to wait. Skier after skier came down the mountain, including the favorite, Katja Seizinger of Germany. The 17th skier, Michaela Dorfmeister, came closest. She skied the course in 1 minute, 18.03 seconds. Her time was a mere one-hundredth of a second (less time than it takes to blink an eye!) slower than Picabo's.

Picabo climbed to the top of the awards podium to accept her gold medal, then spiritedly sang "The Star-Spangled Banner" as the U.S. national anthem played. She was thrilled to add the gold medal to the silver she had won four years earlier. "This gold medal is a dream come true," she said. "Everybody dreams about it. Only so many people can get close to it and make it happen."

11

Picabo shares a lot of the credit for her skiing success with her parents, Dee and Ron.

Always a Handful

Picabo grew up a long, long way from the clamor and glamour of the Olympics. She was born April 3, 1971, in her parents' rural Idaho home. They were miles from any doctor, so the Streets were very worried when Picabo was born and didn't start breathing. Her body was a bright blue color.

Her parents look back at that moment and say Picabo was having her first temper tantrum. But at the time, no one was making jokes. Ron quickly scooped up his daughter and pressed his mouth against hers. He blew into her lungs, and saw her tiny chest rise and fall. Soon she was a healthy pink—and breathing on her own. Ron says Picabo's independent spirit dates from her first minutes of life. "I had to give her her first breath, and I let her go from there," he said.

Dee and Ron Street had gone to Idaho looking for a place where they could raise their children to be free spirits. They found it in a town named Triumph, population 35. The Streets felt their children would learn to rely on themselves in a town so small. They also thought that with so few outside distractions, they could create the tight-knit family of their dreams. Ron worked as a mason, laying bricks and stones; Dee taught music.

Ron's name is actually Roland Wayne Street II, after his father. (His friends call him by a nickname, Stubby.) But he and Dee wanted their children to choose their own names. Picabo's birth certificate says only "Baby Girl" where there should be a name. Her older brother's reads "Baby Boy." Around the house, their parents called them by various nicknames.

Then, when Picabo was about three, the family began planning a trip to Central America. They needed passports, and the government insisted they have proper names on them.

Searching for a name for their young daughter, the Streets looked around at the Idaho landscape. The name of their favorite trout stream (and also a nearby town) was "Picabo," which was translated from the Shoshone and Bannock Indian languages as "shining water," or "silver creek." The Streets thought silver would be a nice image for their young daughter.

The name also fit because as an infant, Picabo had a special fondness for the game of peekaboo. "She loved the game," says Ron. "Any kid any time, any-

14

where in the world will play that game, I've found. Duck back, look out, duck back, look out . . . pretty soon you've got 'em. They trust you."

Picabo thinks there may have been another reason her parents chose the kind of name they did. "They had an idea I was an unusual person and figured, 'She's weird, we might as well give her a strange name,'" Picabo says.

Her brother's official name became Roland Wayne Street III, but people seldom called him that. He went by Baba, or other childhood nicknames like Bubbers, Bubs, or Bobs.

Other kids at school teased Picabo a lot for her unusual name. "I grew up hating my name," she says. But eventually she grew to love the sense of individuality it gave her.

Picabo's childhood was full of freedom—and adventure, too. The trip to Central America when she was three was the first of several trips south her family made to take a break from the long Idaho winters. The trips were also intended to be educational. "The idea was to introduce the kids to as many places and as many people as we could," says Ron.

"We threw these kids in a pickup truck, parked it in Arizona, and dragged them through Mexico and Guatemala on trains," Dee remembers. To many people, Ron and Dee's unusual lifestyle seemed like that of a classic hippie couple. That's not necessarily how they saw themselves, though. Dee makes a distinction between her family and true hippies, who, she says, tended to be unproductive and dependent on drugs. She and Ron always worked hard for what they got. Dee says drugs were never a big deal for her, although Ron admits to smoking marijuana.

Before the children were born, Ron served in the U.S. Marines. Although he later criticized the government's handling of the Vietnam War and joined the peace movement, he remained patriotic. The flag he draped across his shoulders at the Olympics had been on display for years in the Streets' living room.

Because of the way Dee and Ron chose to live, life for Picabo was very different from most of the kids her age. In many ways, she had more in common with kids who grew up in Idaho during the pioneer days of the 1800s. "We had a tough life," Dee remembers. "We had no money. All we did was work. We had a kind of a farm, raised our own chickens and rabbits and cut wood to heat with and cook with.

"In a northern climate, gardening is a challenge," Dee adds. "I made my kids work in the garden. They hated it. But we developed a good relationship out there in that garden."

Picabo seems to agree. "Whenever I think of my childhood," she says, "I think of us doing everything together. We had a real homey atmosphere. We were well taken care of."

Being the only girl among her playmates helped Picabo develop the toughness she needs as a downhill racer.

Growing up in a town as small as Triumph, Picabo faced a very unusual challenge: she was the only girl in the whole town! Only seven of the kids in town were near Picabo's age, and all of them were boys. "We never cut her any slack," says Baba. "She had to earn her spot."

"Once," Picabo remembers, "I got hit in the forehead and knocked out with a baseball, and they just said, 'Ah, c'mon,' and kicked me around and got me back up. So I just had to hack it and be tough. I think that's what made me as tough as I was, growing up in that atmosphere and having the name that I did.

"Kids would ask, 'Do you have a doll?' I'd say, 'No, I have a BB gun.'"

Picabo started skiing when she was five years old.

Her parents say she cried all the way up in the chair lift, afraid she'd fall off the chair as the cable carried it to the top of the mountain. But once she got off the lift, she went zooming off, straight down the hill.

Learning to ski with her father and older brother was a lot like the rough games Picabo played with the boys in Triumph. "I just started chasing my brother and my dad around the mountain," Picabo says. "I had to keep up or get left behind. It was like, 'If you can't keep up, meet us at the car at four o'clock!'"

Dee and Ron have hundreds of stories about young Picabo's outrageous adventures. There was the time she learned to ride a bicycle by climbing on her brother's bike, which had no seat and no brakes. She rolled down the hill in the front yard, crossed the street, and crashed into the neighbor's fence.

"She was always a handful," her mother remembers. At birthday parties, Picabo would sometimes pull out the boxing gloves and "whip the crap out of everybody," says Dee. "She's one of those kinds of people that just has no fear of anything."

Both Picabo and her brother were fearless and full of energy. Faced with such wild children, Ron and Dee knew their best chance was to outsmart them, because they might never be able to control them.

"Our parents never told us what to do. They always explained the consequences and let us make our own decisions," Picabo says. "They let us go out and experiment and were there to pick us up if we fell on our butt."

"We started out a close-knit community of four," says Dee, "and that closeness paid off. We went through a lot of adversity, and we learned we were a team."

Even with the hard work, the Streets took advantage of their rural lifestyle. They owned horses and rode them up into the mountains to camp and fish.

The Streets also didn't own a television set until Picabo was nearly a teenager. Before that, if she wanted to do something fun after supper, she would have to get her older brother or one of her parents to play a game with her. Not having a television just made the family even closer.

"I know I had a different upbringing than a lot of people I ski with," says Picabo, "but at the same time, my family was always big on manners and morals and respect for people. Even though I had a lot of personal freedom, I had a more disciplined life, and I think that's made a difference in my skiing."

Early in her skiing career, Picabo learned music helps her focus on and prepare for a race.

Racing Away

Skiing was a big part of Picabo's life. The Sawtooth Mountain Range was practically in her backyard, and Sun Valley, one of the biggest ski resorts in the country, was just 12 miles away.

When she was only six, Picabo entered and won her first race, organized by Sun Valley for young skiers. Winning that day meant a lot to Picabo, because it showed her that she could do more than just keep up. It showed her that she could be a winner.

Picabo had lots of chances to ski. Twice a week all winter long, her school organized trips to Sun Valley. With every trip down the mountain, Picabo got a little bit faster. Her dad says, "Until she was seven, she followed me. After that, I followed her."

In 1984, when Picabo was turning 13, the Winter Olympic Games took place in Sarajevo, Yugoslavia. Because she had grown up without a television,

Picabo had never seen the Olympics before. But that year, she was watching as five American skiers won medals: Bill Johnson won a gold in the men's down-hill, twin brothers Phil and Steve Mahre finished first and second in the men's **slalom,** and Debbie Armstrong and Christin Cooper won gold and silver in the women's **giant slalom.**

Christin Cooper's silver medal meant the most to Picabo, because they had one thing in common. Cooper was from Ketchum, Idaho, the same small town where Picabo went to elementary school.

Christin Cooper, who lived near Picabo's hometown, races to a silver medal at the 1984 Olympics.

Picabo took her inspiration from Cooper. She has a very clear memory of the day she told her father. "I remember looking up to him and saying, 'Dad, I'm going to win a medal at the Olympics one day.' We caught eyes, and I think he realized I was serious," Picabo remembers. "And he just kind of got this look on his face like, 'Wow, O.K., here we go.' I think he got in his head, 'O.K., if she said that and she means it, then I'm going to be here to make sure I do everything I can to help her get there.'"

Picabo's whole family supported her new goal, but they must have been worried. Picabo had chosen to specialize in the downhill, the most dangerous event in skiing.

There are four major types of **alpine ski racing.** In *slalom* racing, skiers zigzag down two short courses marked by many pairs of closely spaced flags, called gates. In the *giant slalom*, skiers race down two longer courses with more broadly spaced gates. The *Super G* (super giant slalom) is a faster event, still with lots of gates, but spread out over a single long, steep course.

And then there is the *downhill*, the king of them all. Like a giant roller coaster towering above the merry-go-rounds at an amusement park, the downhill is the wildest ride on the mountain. Like the Super G, the course is long and steep, but skiers maneuver around far fewer gates than in other types of races.

With fewer turns to make, the skiers can reach top speed. The few gates placed on the run serve as a safety measure—keeping skiers from going *too* fast or guiding them away from especially dangerous areas.

Every skiing event tests a skier's reflexes and coordination. The downhill tests these, too, but more than anything it tests a skier's raw nerve. The risk of injury is so great, and the margin for error is so small, that skiing the downhill requires a special kind of courage. Fear gets pushed aside, crowded out by pure adrenaline.

GIANT SLALOM

SLALOM

With their emphasis on making tight turns, the slalom and giant slalom are called technical events. In contrast, the Super G and downhill are known as speed events.

Mt. Dick

SUPER
G

DOWNHILL

"To ski the downhill is to defy death every time out," says Andy Mill, a former downhiller who later became a sports commentator on television.

Learning to be a downhill ski racer takes lots of time and effort. Most of the top racers attended special ski academies when they were younger. These academies have regular classes like English and math, but students also get lots of time for physical conditioning and skiing, and they get special instruction from a team of ski coaches.

Despite having little money, Dee and Ron wanted to give Picabo every chance to develop her skiing. When Picabo decided to pursue her Olympic dream, her parents enrolled her in the Rowmark Ski Academy at Salt Lake City, Utah, and moved the family there.

"None of us liked it," Picabo says. "It was a very wealthy school, and I couldn't relate to the other kids in any way. I wanted to be back in Idaho with the hicks who had bare minimum but were happy." Within a year, the family had returned to Idaho, and Picabo was again skiing the slopes at Sun Valley.

Before long, a coach from the U.S. Ski Team, Paul Major, was at Sun Valley and noticed Picabo's skiing. He selected her for the U.S. Junior Team in 1986, when she was 15. A year later, she competed in the World Junior Championships.

Besides time, talent, and dedication, skiing also takes a lot of money—for expenses like lift tickets, ski lessons, special racing equipment, and traveling to races around the country. Picabo's friends, fans, and neighbors chipped in to help pay some of the costs. "We had to go door-to-door one year," her mother says. At times, they even had to scrounge for returnable soda cans to pay for gas.

"Most skiers in this country come from wealthy families," said Major. "Picabo's situation is different, and it's very pleasant to be around her. I love that, to see a kid who worked hard and had a lot of community support."

Community support only went so far, though, and the Streets had to make up the rest on their moderate income. Picabo says she sometimes felt like she was taking more than her share from the family. "The expenses were insane," she says. "But I think the fact that the money didn't come easily made me cherish more what I have, made me work very hard to do my best."

With all of the time Picabo spent traveling and training for races, she eventually dropped out of her public high school. She kept studying on her own though, and earned a general equivalency diploma (GED).

When she was 17, she won the U.S. junior downhill and Super G titles. A knee injury kept her from competing in 1989, but she recovered and skied again on the World Junior Championship Team.

By then, Major and the other coaches felt Picabo was ready to move up from the junior team to the regular team. That meant she would compete against skiers from all over the world for the first time and race on longer, steeper courses. Picabo would be traveling all winter long, from Europe to Japan and around North America. She would be living in hotels and dealing with jet lag.

In Europe, where many competitions take place, skiing is a much more popular sport than it is in the United States. Hundreds or thousands of people attend every race. The crowds make lots of distracting noise, shouting and banging large iron cowbells.

Not only would there be distractions during her runs, but there would be more media coverage of the competitions. Picabo would have to spend time talking to news reporters. She would have to remain focused on her skiing, despite the increased attention. With all of these changes, it's no wonder skiers usually need three to five years to adjust to the world circuit.

Picabo and her coaches also worked to build up her body. She needed to develop the rock-hard legs downhill racers need to power through high-speed turns and absorb the pounding a downhill course delivers. During the race season, which generally runs from December to March, Picabo had to squeeze in workouts when she wasn't traveling or racing. Her hardest workouts, though, took place in the so-called "off season." She did a lot of weight lifting, distance running, and wind sprints. Sometimes her coaches would give her workouts to do on a mountain bike or in-line skates. And sometimes in the summer, the ski team would fly to South America (where it is winter during North American summers) so the team could practice on real snow.

For all the hard physical work, skiing is almost equally a mental challenge. Fortunately, Picabo's mental makeup is rock solid, too. "I think her strength is her ability to convince herself she can do it when it counts," says her teammate, Hilary Lindh. "That's really important, to have that mental strength. Regardless of other people's doubts and concerns, she can still believe in herself."

"She's a heck of a competitor," says Major. "There are a lot better technical skiers out there, but Picabo has the mental strength to pull up every fiber in her body for the win."

The training regimen for alpine skiers like Picabo includes long trail rides on mountain bikes during the summer.

4

Growing Pains

The same strength of mind that helps Picabo win races sometimes works against her. Skiing, like other organized sports, demands team discipline, and coaches have to enforce that discipline. They know if one member of the team messes up, it won't be long before the whole team starts to spin out of control.

The freedom Picabo had enjoyed growing up was making it hard for her to fit in on the team. "My parents taught me to think for myself, to question things," she said. Picabo didn't understand why she had to follow so many orders.

In her first years on the team, Picabo always seemed to be messing up. She complained about having to do the workouts, and she tried to get out of as many team responsibilities as she could. "I never liked having anyone tell me what to do, which the team always seemed to be doing," she said.

When she didn't follow the rules, her coaches tried to rein her in. "Once, we had a 10 P.M. curfew," Picabo recalls, "and when I finally sneaked in, around 1 A.M., there was this note on the door from [Paul Major] telling me not to bother to put my skis on the next day."

"There are a thousand stories," Major says. "So many bad things I don't want to talk about them. Missing meetings, coming in late, leaving early, just coming to camp in terrible shape."

Besides her coaches, there were other people on the U.S. Ski Team that Picabo had a hard time getting along with. A rivalry between Picabo and Hilary Lindh created tension on the team for years and constantly distracted the two from their skiing.

Hilary was two years older than Picabo and had been on the team far longer. Hilary won her first national title in the downhill in 1986, the year Picabo joined the junior team. Picabo hated coming in second to anyone, and it didn't help that she and Hilary were so different from each other. "Our personalities are very different, almost as opposite as you can get," Picabo says. Where Picabo is talkative and outgoing, Hilary is quieter, more reserved.

Hilary says, "I hate being characterized as the strong, silent type. But I've always disliked people who are overbearing, people who have to make an impression by being loud."

While Picabo loves racing, she hasn't always been easy to coach.

Her Pimp

Picabo had a bad attitude toward training, her rivalry with Hilary was making the whole team uneasy, and she wasn't winning any races. Not surprisingly, several coaches wanted her off the team. But Paul Major stuck up for her, in spite of what he described as "an ongoing fight between her and me." One day, Picabo skied badly, threw a temper tantrum in front of the news cameras, and spewed a long string of profanities. Major told a reporter, "There is no filter between her head and her mouth."

Major believed Picabo could be a champion, if only she could learn to control herself. He also respected her as a person, in spite of his coaching problems with her. "At first I didn't know whether she was a block-head," he says. "She's not. She's stubborn, but she's street-smart, and she reads people better than anyone I've been around. She's extremely extroverted. She just loves to tell you what's on her mind. There's nothing contrived about her. She may not have all the social graces to go with it, but you're really seeing a person."

Picabo knew her outrageous personality was one of her strengths, but it was also her biggest problem. She once got some advice from Tamara McKinney, who had won more World Cup races than any other American woman. McKinney told Picabo, "You've got this incredible fire. The day you learn to channel that fire, you're going to be unbeatable."

Picabo's trouble with the team came to a head at the start of summer training camp in 1990. The team trainers had given her a program of exercises to strengthen her injured knee. But when she showed up for training camp, it was obvious that she hadn't done the exercises. In fact, she was completely out of shape. It was the last straw. "I showed up with a bad attitude at camp, and they said, 'O.K., fine, you're out of here. Go home and figure out what you want to do,'" Picabo says.

Stunned, 19-year-old Picabo went home to Idaho. At the time, her family was living in Hawaii, where her father had taken a masonry job. So Picabo stayed at a friend's house and tried to sort out her life. "I was going through a teenage crisis," she said, looking back on that time. "I was having trouble deciding what to do with my life. I wanted to be a normal kid."

Picabo needed time away from the ski team to regain her love for competition and the dedication it required of her.

She was tired of the regimented life of the ski team, tired of "being away from home, being away from family, going to bed early at night, eating right—just everything." When she called her parents, she told them she'd just left the team temporarily because she was sick.

They found out the truth soon enough. One day her father called and ordered Picabo to fly to Hawaii on the double. From the sound of his voice, she knew she was in trouble.

Picabo soon realized Hawaii was going to be more like a Marine boot camp than a tropical paradise. Her father had her doing 50 sit-ups and 100 push-ups before breakfast, then wind sprints and swimming, then more sit-ups and push-ups. While she did them, he held a stopwatch and yelled at her to do them faster. She cursed at him in rage. "Hate me now, thank me later," Ron Street said.

Mornings and evenings, Picabo did workouts under her father's supervision, and all day long she was his assistant on the masonry job. Her task: hauling rocks around the work site. At night she got to rest and think about her future. For three months that was Picabo's life. Somewhere along the way, the bad side of being a professional athlete stopped looking so bad.

"I sat down and wrote out the pros and cons of being a ski racer, and the pros outweighed the cons by a lot," she said.

The ski team was willing to take her back, but only as a member of the junior team. Her coaches noticed a big difference in her attitude this time around. "The talent always was there. Now she has the effort as well," said Major.

Picabo made an effort to train harder—and to control her emotions more. It was a constant battle for her. "There's a little tiger in me that comes out of the middle of nowhere that I really don't have control of sometimes," she admits. "I used to freak out whenever I didn't ski as well as I wanted to. I'd just throw my stuff around, throw a little temper tantrum. I've learned you can't do that."

Despite her troubles with the team, Picabo continued to race and to refine her skiing skills.

Picabo soars over the slope during a 1992 competition.

She couldn't change her basic personality, but she had come to see things in a new light. In Hawaii, she says, "I realized that skiing was a job and I'd better start doing it. It's a fun job, but day in and day out it's still a job.

"My father set me straight," she says. "I was wandering astray. I came back knowing what I wanted to do."

That same year, Picabo won the North American Championship title—the highest level of competition for members of the junior team. The next year, 1992, she won the North American title again. Her victory felt a little hollow, though, because 1992 was the year her old teammate, Hilary Lindh, won a silver medal at the Olympics in Albertville, France.

Her attitude toward Hilary was one thing that Picabo's time in Hawaii hadn't changed. Something about Hilary's calm, controlled manner just drove her crazy. After she was allowed to rejoin the U.S. Ski Team for the 1993 season, Picabo and Hilary went through a whole training camp without speaking a single word to each other.

Hooker Huge

Picabo and a friend celebrate a good run.

On Top of the Mountain

In the world of sports, nothing compares to the Olympic Games, where athletes from more than 100 countries compete for gold, silver, and bronze medals. The Summer and Winter Olympics usually are held every four years, but recently there were Winter Olympics two years apart—in 1992 and 1994.

The Olympics are just one of several levels of ski competition. The Alpine World Championships take place every other year, with gold, silver, and bronze medals awarded, just like in the Olympics. But only alpine events are featured—none of the other winter sports. Many countries, including the United States, also sponsor their own championship events.

For ski racers, the most important races are World Cup races. These are the only races that count toward a skier's ranking throughout the season. There are usually nine World Cup races held throughout the year. The skier with the most points in his or her event wins the World Cup title for that event.

Picabo's first real breakthrough came at the 1993 World Championships in Japan. She won a silver medal in the combined, an event that takes a skier's combined score from races in the downhill and slalom events. She was 22 years old and had devoted the last seven years of her life to skiing.

"It kind of surprised me a little," Picabo said after she had won the medal, "but I could feel that next step coming on. I didn't know if it would happen here or a little later."

Major watched her at the awards ceremony and observed, "Being up on the podium was like tasting candy to her. She's going to do what it takes to get back up there."

It didn't take her long. At the U.S. Championships later that season, she won a gold in the Super G, a silver in the combined, and a bronze in the downhill. "It's all starting to come together for me," she said excitedly. "I'm ready for it mentally, and I'm ready for it physically."

The next big hurdle for Picabo was winning a World Cup race. Then, in a 1994 race in Germany, Picabo held a commanding lead with most of the racers' results in. Picabo was watching her competitors' runs on a video monitor, becoming more excited and happy by the minute.

The ski racing world took notice when Picabo took second in the World Championships. The ski team sent Picabo to the race mostly so she could gain experience, but Picabo also gained a medal.

The 32nd skier to run the course that day was Ulrike Maier, a friendly Austrian woman Picabo had come to know well over the years. Picabo watched the monitor in horror as Maier suddenly lost her balance, swerved off the course, and crashed into a padded post. The impact snapped Maier's neck, killing her instantly.

Picabo saw a helicopter take Maier's body away. Then the weather changed, and by the time the race was restarted, the snow was much colder—and faster—for the later skiers. Picabo eventually came in seventh, but winning a World Cup race didn't seem so important by then.

Three weeks later, Picabo was in Lillehammer, Norway, for the 1994 Olympics. Reporters from thousands of newspapers covered the Olympics, and the Olympic races were televised around the globe.

Picabo carves a turn on the Olympic course.

Picabo proved she would be a contender when she posted the top time in a practice run on the downhill course. Then, on the day of the race, she had a terrific run and finished just behind Katja Seizinger of Germany. She had won a silver medal! Her unexpected finish, combined with her fascinating upbringing, captured the attention of reporters. Picabo enjoyed being in the spotlight, although she knew better than to let herself think the Olympics had changed anything. "I wanted to suck up my medal, do the talk shows," she said. "But then I realized I still had a season left. I was like, 'This is serious. Who cares if you have a medal?'"

As a young girl growing up in Idaho, Picabo dreamed of winning an Olympic medal in skiing.

When the World Cup tour was over, Picabo had finished among the top 15 skiers in four downhill races. She also had a strong showing in the U.S. Championships, winning the downhill and finishing second in the Super G.

In 1995, the women's team had a new coach, Herwig Demschar. He had coached the powerful Austrian team until he resigned after Ulrike Maier's fatal accident. When Demschar arrived, he didn't like the lingering rivalry between Picabo and Hilary.

"Hilary is a very strong person and as an athlete takes a back seat to no one," Demschar said. "But Picabo commands so much attention. It's hard for Hilary, hard for everyone." Before the season started, he told each of them, "You guys are affecting the whole team when you're like this."

The ice between the two racers didn't start to thaw, though, until the season was under way. The breakthrough came at a race in France. "We just sat down and talked things out and decided this was hurting us both," Hilary said. "Basically, we both started skiing better when we decided to get along. I'm impressed with what Picabo did, what we did together."

"I think we both realized that it wasn't in our best interests to be at each other's throats," Picabo said. "I've emulated [copied] some of her traits, and it's made me a more rounded person and racer... She's been more of a role model for me than she'll ever know."

Picabo and Hilary Lindh needed to patch up their relationship before they both could become elite skiers.

Picabo started the 1995 season with an unusual display of modesty. "I'm absolutely nowhere on the World Cup," she said before the season's first downhill in Colorado. "Just because I won an Olympic silver medal, that doesn't mean jack, really."

She proved her point the same day by wiping out early in the course. She somersaulted down the slope and tore a ligament in her hand while trying to stop herself. Hilary rushed over and asked, "Peek, you O.K.?" Picabo gave her a hug.

Picabo fell during this race in Vail, Colorado, but she was happy when Hilary won.

Hilary won that day's race, but Picabo found a silver lining in her own disastrous performance. "When you take a big digger [fall] and walk away from it, it can give you more confidence than anything in the world," she said.

It must have worked that way, because Picabo won the season's next World Cup race. What's more, she went on to win six out of nine World Cup downhills that year.

"The first one blew my mind," she says. After winning her second, she called the victory premature. Even after winning an unbelievable five World Cup races in a row, she insisted, "I was lucky." Her coaches and teammates were amazed—by her skiing and by her modesty. This didn't sound anything like the brash, overconfident Picabo they had known.

As the season wore on, Picabo's victories piled up. Before Picabo's extraordinary season, 11 years had passed since the last time a woman from the United States had won a World Cup downhill race. As recently as 1994, some officials of the U.S. Skiing Association had proposed eliminating the women's downhill program altogether, because they saw no chance that the women's team would ever be competitive again.

Coming into the last downhill race of the season, Picabo was so far ahead in the standings that she had already clinched the title. But instead of coasting, she hustled down the hill and won the race.

The following day, she entered what was to be the last Super G of the season. Halfway down the course, she lost her balance at 60 miles per hour and fell forward. She landed first on her upper back. "And then after that, I closed my eyes and tumbled for a ways," she remembers. She fell several hundred yards down the mountain, smashed into a pair of skis, then finally came to a stop on her right side.

She lay on the snow for 15 minutes, as medical

personnel put her neck in a brace. From her stretcher, before being taken to the hospital by helicopter, she radioed advice about the course to Hilary, who was preparing to make her run. Picabo's injury turned out to be minor, but she had finished her season in real style!

Later, Picabo was presented with a crystal globe for winning the 1995 World Cup downhill title. "I didn't know what my reaction would be, but as soon as I held it I started crying immediately. Crying and laughing at the same time," Picabo said. She became the first non-European, woman or man, in the history of downhill skiing to win the title outright.

Hilary had finished second overall, with two downhill gold medals and one silver. Hers would have been the best finish in a decade for a U.S. woman—had it not been for Picabo's miracle year.

The 1996 season brought with it a very different set of expectations for Picabo. As the champion, she was the skier to beat, the person everyone was watching. "I know it's a new ball game this year and I have to prepare as hard as anyone, maybe harder," she said during the team's summer training camp. "It's scary on one hand, but this sort of challenge is right up my alley. I've got huge bull's-eyes on my back. Catch me if you can!"

Nobody could. When the 1996 season was over, Picabo was again the World Cup downhill champion.

She felt a little discouraged, though, because she'd won only three races, instead of six.

Her mother had to give her a reality check. "I had to explain that a down year for her is a killer season for anyone else," Dee said. What about the fact that Picabo had placed second or third in almost every race she hadn't won? What about her gold medal in the World Championships downhill, the first for an American?

"It took me a while, but I've come to terms with the fact that I'll probably never top last year or even match it," she acknowledged. Picabo had learned that success takes getting used to—in some unexpected ways.

In Bormio, Italy, Picabo finished a fabulous 1995 season.

On her way to yet another win, Picabo applauds her time at
the 1996 World Cup race in Lake Louise, Alberta.

Enjoying the View

In Hawaii, Picabo had learned that skiing was a job. As she rose to the top of the skiing profession, she found out that skiing is also big business. "There are a lot of demands for appearances and endorsements," she said. For instance, a company might pay her several thousand dollars to use its products and pose for pictures. Or she could earn money by signing autographs and chatting with customers for a couple of hours. It was fun at first, but after a while, she could see these activities were crowding out her skiing schedule.

Picabo has a long and ever-changing list of sponsors and endorsement deals. She has endorsed ski equipment, training videos, ski resorts, lip balm, soft drinks, household products, and clothing. Her 1995 World Cup title helped her earn close to half a million dollars. Only a fraction of that was prize money from the races she'd won.

Sometimes Picabo combines work and play, like when she competed on the television show *American Gladiators*. She also appeared on *Sesame Street*, where she and Elmo played a game of (can you guess?) peekaboo!

After her success in 1996, Picabo headed into the 1997 season in great shape and primed to make a run at her third straight downhill title. She had a strong run in her first race of the season. Then disaster struck.

Picabo convinced Sesame Street muppet Elmo that she was an Olympic medalist in skiing—and not in the game of peekaboo, as he thought.

Photo courtesy Don Perdue/CTW

Picabo's 1997 season came to a premature end when she tore knee ligaments in a fall during the second race of the year.

During a practice run at Vail, Colorado, she lost her balance while airborne. She landed hard, tearing ligaments in her left knee. She had surgery within a week, then spent the better part of a year working the knee back into shape.

Even before she could resume skiing, Picabo had a trainer ski down the Olympic course, carrying her on his back. She needed to see the course first-hand to plot her strategy for racing it. "It was very important for me to visualize the courses, to put them deep in my mind, to become familiar with the whole environment," she said. "I could see the course in my mind, and it helped me to stay focused. Knowing what I was fighting for made my rehabilitation easier."

When Picabo returned to the circuit in December 1997, she consistently improved. In January, a month before the Olympics, she took fourth on a downhill course in Italy.

Then came the crash. A faulty binding caused one of Picabo's skis to fall off during a race in Sweden. She crashed into a safety fence and lost consciousness briefly. When she came to, she was distressed that her favorite ski, which she had named Junior, was broken.

Picabo won an Olympic gold medal in her next race, but proof that her injuries still haunted her came days later in the Olympic downhill race. Downhill racers depend on their memory as much as their strong legs and quick reflexes. Moving at more than 70 miles per hour, they are skiing so fast that they have to start turning even before the curves come into sight. They have no room for mistakes and no time to react to surprises. With course conditions very different from her practice run, Picabo couldn't make herself attack. She placed a respectable sixth, however. "I've hit too many fences this year," she said. "I didn't want to push the envelope. To me, it wasn't worth risking my health to win another medal."

But a few weeks later, while skiing in Switzerland, Picabo fell during a downhill race and broke her left leg in several places. At first, Picabo thought about retiring from skiing. But later, she told a reporter that she might return for the Olympics in 2002.

The 2002 Winter Olympic Games will be held in Salt Lake City, Utah. "I can't see myself missing the Olympics when the opportunity is there on your home turf," she said. Picabo said her injuries would certainly cause her to miss all of the 1999 season.

Even if she never competes again, Picabo will have left her mark. At Sun Valley, Picabo's home ski resort, there is a section of the mountain called "Picabo's Run." In two different towns in Idaho, you can drive a car down "Picabo Street."

Picabo may add to her Olympic medal collection.

Picabo is also using her fame and fortune to benefit others. She gives 10 percent of her World Cup earnings to organizations that support youth programs. She helps raise money for many other charities, including the Women's Sports Foundation.

Picabo lives in her own home just outside Portland, Oregon, after living in Idaho with her family until she was 23. Her family is still a big part of her life, though. "My parents have been very supportive," she says. "My father gives me the 'I don't care how you do, I love you anyway.' My mother organizes everything. And my brother, Bubba, is always there."

Picabo realizes she's not just a role model for other young skiers. "While I was in Washington, D.C., we Olympians spoke at inner-city schools," she said. "The kids I talked to didn't know much about skiing, but they said, 'I know you. I watched you on TV!'" Picabo sets an example for everyone because of who she is, and how she got to the top of the skiing world.

"Sports are an avenue to being happy with myself," she says, "and that's why I do the media I do. I'm in the prime place to be a role model and inspiration for the country's youth, and I'm jumping on it."

She also realizes she has something to say to young girls. Picabo learned some hard lessons growing up as the only girl in town, and she wants to pass them along. "It's important for girls to see bigger women with strong opinions, who are also sensitive and vulnerable. I want to tell them, 'You can be a strong athlete and still be feminine,'" she said. "But most of all, my goal is to have fun at what I'm doing. That's when you'll always be the most successful." And if anyone has ever had fun *and* success, it would be a skier named Picabo Street.

Career Highlights

World Cup Circuit

Season	Downhill World Cup Ranking	Downhill Races Won	Downhill Top 5 Finishes	Super G Races Won	Super G Top 5 Finishes	Overall World Cup Ranking
1993	18	0	0	0	0	39
1994	8	0	2	0	0	36
1995	1	6	8	0	2	5
1996	1	3	7	0	1	6
1997	25*	0	1	0	0	71*
1998	17	0	1	0	0	46
Totals		9	19	0	3	

Career Honors
- Gold medal in Olympic Super G, 1998.
- Gold medal in World Championships downhill, 1996.**
- Gold medal in U.S. Championships downhill, 1994, 1996.
- Gold medal in U.S. Championships Super G, 1993, 1996.
- Silver medal in Olympic downhill, 1994.
- Silver medal in World Championships combined, 1993.
- Silver medal in U.S. Championships Super G, 1994.
- Silver medal in U.S. Championships combined, 1993.
- Bronze medal in World Championships Super G, 1996.
- Bronze medal in U.S. Championships downhill, 1991, 1993.
- United States Olympic Committee's Sportswoman of the Year, 1995.

* Standings for 1997 include only the one race Picabo completed before sustaining her season-ending injury.
** World Championship races were postponed from 1995 because of poor weather.

Glossary

alpine ski racing: Timed competitions held on steep mountain ski runs. Alpine races are held separately from other ski competitions, such as nordic events that include ski jumping and cross-country skiing.

downhill: A type of alpine racing in which skiers race once down a long course (at least 500 meters of vertical drop for women) marked by few gates. Speeds can easily exceed 70 miles per hour.

gates: Obstacles through which skiers must turn. In slalom races, gates consist of two single poles with triangular flags. In the other disciplines, each gate is a set of two poles with a rectangular panel hung between them. Gates in slalom, giant slalom, and Super G alternate between red and blue, but only red gates are used in downhill races.

giant slalom: A type of alpine racing in which skiers race through gates set on a course. Giant slalom differs from slalom because it has a longer course (at least 250 meters of vertical drop) with greater spacing between fewer gates. Times for two different runs are combined to determine the event's winner.

gliding: Skiing through the flat, relatively straight parts of a run. Gliding is done on the bottoms of the skis, unlike turning, which is done using the edges.

slalom: A type of alpine racing in which skiers negotiate a relatively short course (120 meters of vertical drop) and make turns through at least 42 closely spaced gates. Results are based on combined times of two separate runs.

Super G: A type of alpine skiing that combines elements of the giant slalom and downhill. Super G courses for women typically have 30 widely spaced gates over a course with 350 meters or more of vertical drop.

tuck: A posture in which a skier folds down his or her body so it can cut through the air as quickly as possible. When Picabo is in a good tuck, she positions her feet slightly more than shoulder width apart, with her hands close together in front of her chin and with her elbows pulled in.

Sources

Information for this book was obtained from: Harvey Araton *(The New York Times*, 20 February 1994, 11 February 1998, 16 February 1998); Christopher Clarey *(The New York Times*, 23 January 1998); Christin Cooper *(Skiing*, September 1995); George Diaz *(Chicago Tribune*, 20 February 1994); John Dostal *(Skiing*, December 1996) Chris Dufresne *(Los Angeles Times*, 26 February 1993, 8 February 1994, 20 February 1994); Michael Farber *(Sports Illustrated*, 19 December 1994, 18 December 1995, 29 February 1996); Robert Frohlich *(Alpine World*, Summer 1995); Brendan Hanrahan *(Chicago Tribune*, 8 February 1994); Stephen Harris *(The Boston Globe*, 20 February 1994); Philip Hersh *(Chicago Tribune*, 26 January 1995); William Oscar Johnson *(Sports Illustrated*, 28 February 1994); Ron Judd *(The Seattle Times*, 16 March 1995); Curry Kirkpatrick *(Newsweek*, 14 February 1994); Chantal Knapp *(Women's Sports & Fitness News*, July 1994); Patrick Lang *(SkiNet*, 12 February 1998); Tim Layden *(Newsday*, 20 February 1994); Barbara Lloyd *(The New York Times*, 18 February 1993, 20 February 1993, 16 November 1995, 14 March 1998); Bob Lochner *(Los Angeles Times*, 17 February 1995); Sarah Love *(Mountain Zone News*, 18 December 1997); John Meyer *(Rocky Mountain News*, 2 December 1994); Charlie Meyers *(The Sporting News*, 14 February 1994); *The Denver Post*, 2 December 1994, 13 February 1994, 20 February 1994, 15 November 1995; Dan Moffett *(The Palm Beach Post*, 22 February 1994); *The New York Times*, 20 April 1994; Peter Oliver *(Skiing*, January 1994); Angus Phillips *(The Washington Post*, 20 February 1994); Stephen Porino *(Ski Racing Online*, 11 February 1998); Susan Reed and Tom Cunneff *(People Weekly*, 7 February 1994); Bob Ryan *(The Boston Globe*, 20 February 1994); *Ski Magazine*, September 1995; Allen St. John *(Ski Trade News*, November 1994); The United States Ski Association's website; (Alexander Wolff and Christian Stone *(Sports Illustrated*, 27 March 1995); and Steve Woodward *(USA Today*, 14 April 1994).

Index

Write to Picabo

You can send mail to Picabo at the address on the right. If you write a letter, don't get your hopes up too high. Picabo and other athletes get lots of letters every day, and they aren't always able to answer them all.

Picabo Street
United States Skiing Association
PO Box 100
Park City UT 84060

Acknowledgments

Photographs and illustrations are reproduced by permission of: Sports File/Tim Hancock, pp. 1, 20, 29, 38, 45, 48, 51; © ALLSPORT USA/Mike Powell, pp. 2–3, 11, 43, 52; © ALLSPORT USA/ Jamie Squire, p. 6; © ALLSPORT USA/AFLO, p. 9; SportsChrome East/ West, Bernd Lauter, p. 12; © ALLSPORT USA/Simon Bruty, pp. 17, 44; © ALLSPORT USA/Steve Powell, p. 22; Laura Westlund and Michael Tacheny, pp. 24–25; Sports File/Scott Smith, pp. 30, 37; Sports File/Scott Markewitz, p. 33; Sports File/Lee Wardle, p. 35; Sports File/Heather Black, pp. 40, 55; © ALLSPORT USA/Nathan Bilow, pp. 47, 57; Don Perdue/CTW, p. 54.

Front cover photograph by © ALLSPORT USA/ZOOM.
Back cover photograph by © ALLSPORT USA/Mike Powell.

About the Author

Joel Dippold has six pairs of skis—for water-skiing, cross-country skiing, alpine skiing, and ski mountaineering—but he has promised his mother he'll never take up downhill racing. He lives in Portland, Oregon (Picabo's new hometown) and has also written *Troy Aikman: Quick-Draw Quarterback.*